Design and Make
MASKS

Susie Hodge

W
FRANKLIN WATTS
LONDON • SYDNEY

Contents

Making masks

This book is all about making masks.
It shows you how to design and make them
with things you can find around your home.
As well as masks for a party, like the scary
monster mask, we also show you how
to create masks from around the world.

Masks through history

Throughout history, people all over the world have used masks to change their appearance. One of the oldest masks dates from between about 10,000 and 12,000 BC. It was found in South America. It is a fossil of a llama's vertebra, carved into the shape of a coyote's head.

Ancient Egyptians wore animal masks, too. They believed they represented the spirits of the dead. The kings of Ancient Egypt, such as Tutankhamun (left), were often buried with very expensive masks.

In some parts of the world, tribal people still use masks to call upon the spirits of the dead. They believe they can help to grow crops and protect them from enemies and illness.

There are also masks for festivals, such as Chinese New Year (left), and for plays, rituals and celebrations like Hallowe'en.

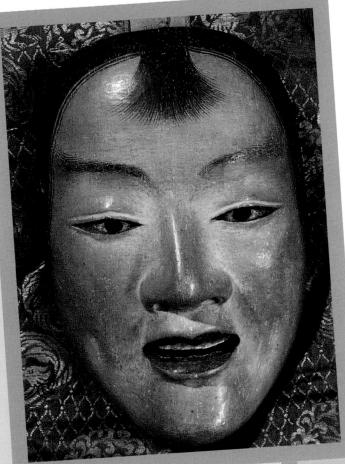

Changing character

Actors and carnival characters use masks to take on new personalities. They can be used to make a person appear frightening, exotic, beautiful, mysterious or funny. In Japan, Noh masks (left) were made for early religious festivals. All the roles in the Japanese Noh theatre were played by men who created their character through the mask and their body movements.

Disguise

People who don't want to be recognised, such as highwaymen and bank robbers, traditionally wore masks, too, to disguise their faces. In many films and television programmes, superheroes wear masks to hide their real identity. Often, children like wearing masks to pretend to be their favourite characters.

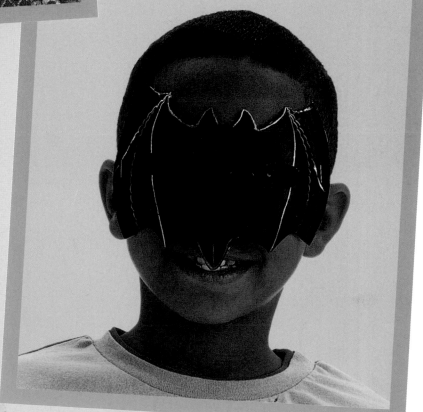

Getting ready

These two pages show you all the different materials and equipment you will need to make the masks in this book. You don't need all of the materials for each mask, but it will be helpful to have them available.

Before you start, gather everything you need and keep it all in a large box or in a tidy corner of your room. Collect some of the materials gradually; there is no need to get everything at once. Here are some suggestions of different materials and equipment you might need, and also a recipe for papier mâché.

Things to collect

A selection of card, cardboard and paper (including tissue and tracing paper) in different sizes, colours and thicknesses

Paper party bowls   Plaster gauze

Old newspapers, cardboard tubes, egg boxes, feathers, bottle tops, cotton reels, paper plates, ribbons, sequins and beads, and silver foil

Paints, especially poster paints, and, if possible, silver and gold or any metallic colours

Hole punch

Scraps of cloth, including felt, calico and other medium-weight fabrics that won't fray easily

Elastic is important, especially thin, hat elastic, used to hold masks on your head

PVA glue is extremely useful for all sorts of masks. It can be used as glue for paper, card and fabric, diluted to make papier mâché and painted over a completed mask to make a varnish.

Balloons, which can be any colour, are useful for building up papier mâché masks, but they must be round and the size of your head when blown up.

A cutting knife and cutting board – always get an adult to help you when using a knife

Paint brushes

Pencils and some felt-tip pens

Double-sided sticky tape and masking tape

Paper or kitchen towels for clearing up and an apron or old shirt to protect your clothing

Scissors

Tape measure

Also collect pipe cleaners, raffia, string and wool

Papier mâché

You will need:
petroleum jelly
newspaper
paint brush
PVA glue
(with a little water added)

Method
Smear some petroleum jelly over the object you are using as a mould. Tear the newspaper into small strips. Layer each strip over the object, painting a generous amount of diluted glue over each strip as you lay it down. Continue doing this until the paper is 2 or 3 mm thick. If you want to create a finer surface, use tissue paper for the top layers. Leave to dry thoroughly before painting or decorating.

Butterfly

This bright butterfly mask is really comfortable to wear. You can make it from thin, flexible card but be careful not to use heavy materials for the decoration or the mask won't stay on properly.

Look at this!

This butterfly mask is part of an elaborate costume worn at the Venice carnival in Italy. Look at the shape of the wings. Butterflies' wings can be different shapes depending on the species.

✱ What shape wings will your butterfly have?

Design and select

It's a good idea to design your butterfly before you begin and plan the different steps. Will you make it from one large piece of card or add separate bits and pieces? How will you decorate it? Select your materials – we've chosen some thin, coloured card, sequins, glitter glue, paints and felt.

Make

1 Draw the shape of the mask, making sure that it is large enough to cover the upper part of your face. Use card that is firm enough to stand up, but flexible enough to curve around your face.

Challenge
How could you add on other features like legs or antennae?

2 Cut all the way around the mask. Make sure that the curved shape over your nose fits comfortably. To mark the eye holes, hold the mask on your nose, feel where your eyes are and gently mark this on the mask with a pencil. Draw round these marks with a bottle top to make the eye holes.

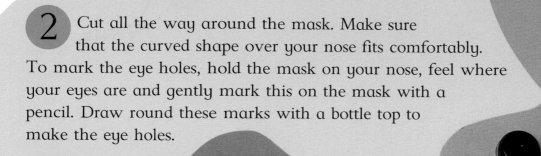

3 Cut out the eye holes by placing the mask on a protected surface and pierce the centre of each eye hole with a sharp pencil point. Get an adult to help you trim around each hole with small, sharp scissors.

4 Cut out shapes for the lower wings. You could use card or felt for these; glue them to the mask. Cut out a head and body for your butterfly and attach to the centre of the mask.

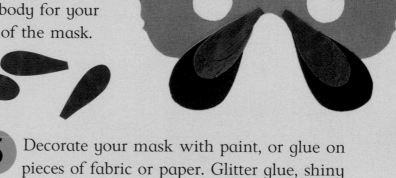

5 Decorate your mask with paint, or glue on pieces of fabric or paper. Glitter glue, shiny paint and sequins are effective. Make a hole in each end of the mask with a hole punch. Poke through some elastic, then tie a knot in each end and secure with sticky tape. If the mask is part of a costume, make sure it matches your outfit.

Challenge
How could you adapt the mask to make a bee instead?

Bat mask

Change a paper party bowl into a bat mask! You will be amazed at how quickly and simply you can do this.

Design and select

Design a bat mask that just covers your eyes and nose. Think about the shape of bats' wings and the circular shape of the bowl you are going to use to make your mask. Draw a picture of your bat mask and decide how you are going to decorate it – with black paint or will you add other colours? Think about how you will hold your mask in place – we're using elastic.

Make

1 Find a paper bowl that is small enough to cover your face, but big enough to curve just around the sides. You could always use a paper plate if a bowl isn't quite big enough.

2 Hold the bowl against your face. Work out where your eyes are and make light pencil marks on the base of the bowl. Draw your bat design on the underside of the bowl, including the eye shapes where you marked your eye positions.

10

3 Get an adult to help you cut out the bat shape. You may need help with the eye holes, too.

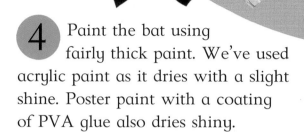

4 Paint the bat using fairly thick paint. We've used acrylic paint as it dries with a slight shine. Poster paint with a coating of PVA glue also dries shiny.

Challenge
We decorated our mask with silver paint. What else could you use to make it glitter?

5 Make a hole on either side of the mask using a hole punch. Thread thin elastic through the holes, tie a knot in each end to hold it in place. Secure it with sticky tape.

Challenge
Could you make a robot mask from the same sort of materials? How would you cut or shape it? Would you stick things on it or paint it?

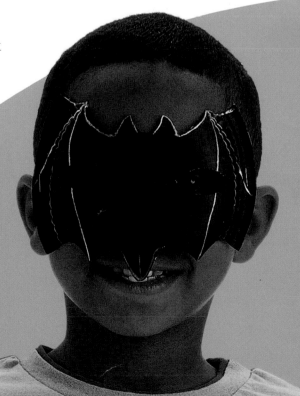

Masquerade mask

Make a glamorous mask that you hold against your face with a stick like they wore at some 18th-century masquerade balls!

Look at this!

In the 18th century, ladies and gentlemen met at special masked balls, wearing masks like this, some held on a stick. They had great fun guessing who was behind the masks when they first arrived. All your friends could make their own versions of these masks for a fancy dress or masquerade party.

Design and select

Think about what you will use for the mask, the stick and the decorations and draw a picture of your idea. Select your materials — we've used silver card, a straw, glitter, sequins, metallic paint, feathers and felt.

Make

1 Draw your mask shape and cut it out. Make sure it is big enough to cover your eyes well and a bit wider than your face.

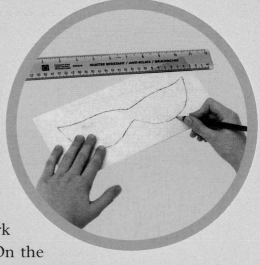

2 Hold the mask up to your face and gently feel where your eyes are and mark lightly in pencil. On the back of your mask, draw round a small coin to make the shape for the eyes.

12

3 Get an adult to help you carefully cut out the eye holes using sharp scissors. Now, using sticky tape, attach a straw to the side of the back of the mask.

Challenge

How could you decorate the straw so that it matches the glamorous mask? Perhaps add some ribbon or tinsel.

4 Begin to decorate your mask. It can be as elaborate as you like, made up from different shapes and patterns. Tip: it's a good idea to try to make each side the same.

5 You will have used a lot of glue to decorate the mask, which will take a long time to dry, so put it somewhere safe for about 24 hours. Make sure it's nowhere near family members who might smudge it, or even pets who might walk on it!

Challenge

How could you adapt this mask to cover your whole face? Try using a bigger piece of card and decorating it all over, using sequins, beads and feathers.

13

Tiger

A tiger mask comes alive when you make it with parts of the face projecting forward.

Design and select

Design a tiger mask that has parts sticking out to make it look more realistic. Find a picture of a tiger to work out the pattern of the markings. Draw a picture of your idea and then choose the materials you will use. We used some orange card, white, black, red and green paint, glue, staples, sticky tape and elastic.

Make

1 Cut out the card shape for the main part of the face (right), large enough to cover your own face. You'll make the ears, nose and mouth from separate bits of card. Draw tiger markings and two eyes on it. See page 9 for how to cut out the eye holes.

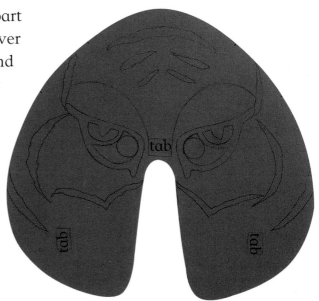

2 Mark where the ears will go on the edge of the mask. Also mark where you will attach the nose and mouth tabs.

3 To make the ears, fold a rectangular piece of card in half. Draw the ear shape (shown on the left) on one side and then cut out both ear shapes at the same time.

14

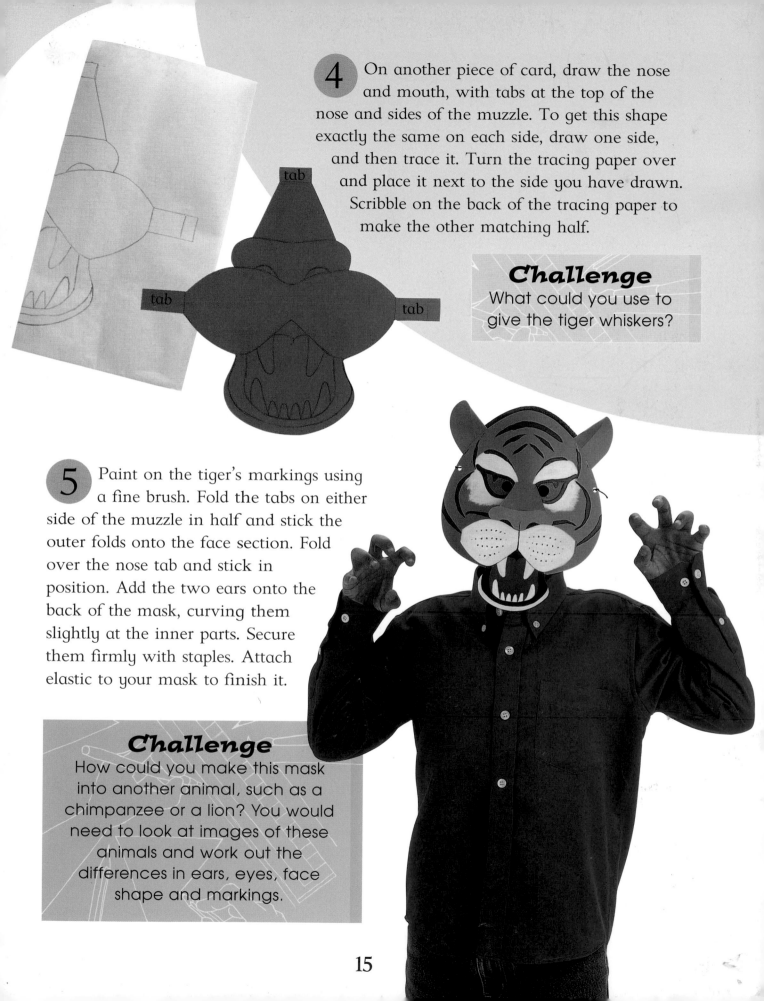

4 On another piece of card, draw the nose and mouth, with tabs at the top of the nose and sides of the muzzle. To get this shape exactly the same on each side, draw one side, and then trace it. Turn the tracing paper over and place it next to the side you have drawn. Scribble on the back of the tracing paper to make the other matching half.

tab

tab

tab

Challenge
What could you use to give the tiger whiskers?

5 Paint on the tiger's markings using a fine brush. Fold the tabs on either side of the muzzle in half and stick the outer folds onto the face section. Fold over the nose tab and stick in position. Add the two ears onto the back of the mask, curving them slightly at the inner parts. Secure them firmly with staples. Attach elastic to your mask to finish it.

Challenge
How could you make this mask into another animal, such as a chimpanzee or a lion? You would need to look at images of these animals and work out the differences in ears, eyes, face shape and markings.

15

Talking pirate

Make your mask come to life
with a mouth that moves!

Design and select

What talking character will you create?
You could make a pirate like we have. Think
about what your pirate will look like — will he
be angry or smiling? Draw a picture of your idea
and then select your materials. We've chosen
thin cream-coloured card, paints, a small wooden
stick and thin elastic.

Make

1 Based on your pirate drawing, create
   a 'face' shape on your card. Use your face
to work out the right size.

2 Copy your pirate's face onto the
   cut out card face; making sure
that you put the eyes in the right place.
(Check this by holding the card 'face'
against your own face and gently feel
where your eyes are).

16

3 Cut off the chin in a curved line.

4 Tape the stick to the centre of the back of this chin and mouth part. Attach two oval shapes to the back of the chin (right) and make two folds in them, as shown (left), to make the hinges. Attach the top of these to the back of the face part.

5 Paint the mask in flesh colours. Peach, white and brown make a good pirate skin colour. Use more or less brown for darker or lighter skin. Get an adult to help cut out the two eye holes. Add some white for the eye and mix white with blue for the bandana. To make it look like real, creased fabric, add some stripes in darker and lighter blue. Paint the eye patch black.

Challenge
How could you change your mask so the pirate is wearing a hat?

6 Staple elastic to each side of the mask to hold it on your head.

Challenge
What could you use to make the hair look more realistic?

Monster

You can turn yourself into a monster with a cardboard box! Using the box's corner creates an instant 3D effect.

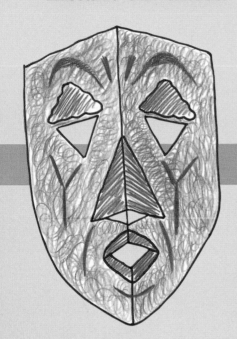

Look at this!

In February, all over the world Chinese communities celebrate their New Year by dressing up in large dragon costumes and masks and dancing through the streets.

✳ Why do you think the dragons are so colourful?

Design and select

Design a monster mask with built-up features using a box as a base. Draw a picture of your idea. Select your materials to build up the mask's features. We've used spare card from the box, kitchen paper turned into papier mâché, and paint. You'll need to decorate the mask too — colourful paint works well.

Make

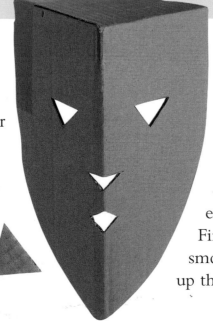

1 Based on your sketch, draw your monster's head on a corner of the cardboard box, including eyes, nose and mouth. Make sure it is big enough to cover your face. Ask an adult to help you cut it out.

2 Using the spare cardboard, cut out pieces to build up the features. Cut out two small triangles to fit over each eye and two larger triangles for either side of the nose. Finally, you need four small shapes to build up the lips.

3 Glue these shapes onto your mask and give the whole thing a coating of yellow paint. (This is an undercoat. If your monster is going to be blue, give the mask an undercoat of white or blue so that the brown card doesn't show through.)

4 Now tear up pieces of kitchen paper. Dip these into a mixture of PVA glue and water and scrunch them onto areas that you want to build up even more, such as the nose and eyelids. Leave the mask in a warm place to dry thoroughly.

5 Paint the mask in vivid monster-like colours, using a different colour for the features. Try red or white on blue, black on green or yellow on purple. Staple a strong piece of elastic to either side of your mask to go round your head. Put your mask on and make monster noises!

Challenge
Monster masks can be frightening and so can ghost and skull masks. Could you make a skull mask in a similar way to this one? How would you create the face?

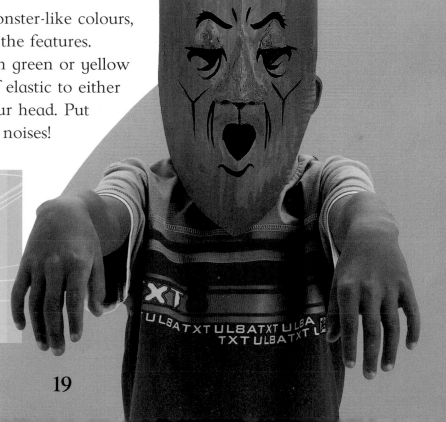

19

Feathery friend

An exotic bird mask can be used for dances, parties or just for playing in!

Design and select

Look at some pictures of colourful birds and design a bird mask based on one of them. Draw it on paper and use anything you have in the house to make it. We've used card, glue, elastic and coloured paper.

Make

1 Make your mask so that it fits the size and shape of your head. Cut out a simple mask shape. Get an adult to help you cut out two eye shapes using sharp scissors.

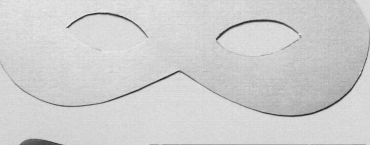

Challenge

How could you include a beak on the main mask shape rather than adding it separately?

2 To make the beak, first fold a square piece of card in half. Draw a line diagonally from one corner to the other and cut along it. Fold this triangle in half and cut a small split from the bottom of the fold, as shown above, to make two flaps. These will be folded over and stuck to the mask (see page 21).

3 Stick the beak onto the main mask. You may need to staple this on as well as using glue or sticky tape to ensure that it holds securely.

4 Cut out some different sized feather shapes in different coloured papers.

Challenge
What other material could you use to make the feathers?

5 Glue on the paper feathers, matching colour for colour on either side. Put the bigger feathers on the outer sides of the mask and the smaller feathers around the eyes. Layer them on top of each other leaving the top half loose, like real feathers. Attach some elastic to the mask. Cover your beak with yellow paper.

Challenge
How could you make a mask with a longer or different-shaped beak and longer, curling strips of paper to look like long, ruffled feathers?

Japanese Noh mask

Masks have been worn in theatres for thousands of years. Noh masks were made for religious festivals in Japan.

Look at this!

All the roles in the Japanese Noh theatre were played by men who underwent long training in the art. They created their character through the mask and their body movements.

✱ What sort of character do you think this mask would be?

✱ Does the face look realistic?

Design and select

Design a copy of an ancient Noh mask with a face full of character. Will you choose a happy character, or a more serious face? Select your materials – we've used papier mâché moulded on a balloon and paint.

Make

1 Blow up a balloon, until it's about the size of your head.

2 Now you need to use papier mâché to make the base of the mask (see page 7 for a recipe). Cover one side of the balloon with the papier mâché to create a face shape.

3 Leave the papier mâché to dry – this will take at least 24 hours. Once the mask is fully dry, you can burst the balloon!

4 You will be left with the mask shape ready to paint. Hold it against your face, feel where your mouth and eyes are and mark the place with a pencil. Get an adult to help cut them out. Make the nose (shown below) by adding on some more papier mâché and moulding it to the right shape.

Challenge
How could you adapt the face and features to make it look like an old man or woman?

5 Paint your mask using creamy colours for the skin (you could mix white with a touch of yellow ochre or orange) and pick out the features in black and red. Attach elastic at eye level, either stapling this on (knot it first) or piercing a hole on each side and tying it round. Varnish with a layer of PVA glue to make the mask shine.

Challenge
See if you can find any other masks used in theatres around the world and make your own version of them using the same techniques.

Majestic mask

Sometimes you can give a mask character by giving it a headdress or hat. A crown and beard tell you that this is a king.

Design and select

How will you make your mask?
Will it be a king or queen? What kind of facial features will it have? Design your character and then select your materials. We've chosen thin card, paint, glitter glue and sequins.

Make

1 Draw your mask design on the card. Cut out the shape of the face, including the shape of the crown. Get an adult to help you draw on the eyes, nose and mouth and cut them out. On either side of the nose, mark on two small lines where you will make vertical slits to attach the nose to the mask.

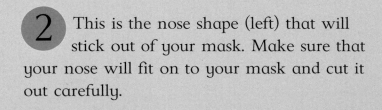

2 This is the nose shape (left) that will stick out of your mask. Make sure that your nose will fit on to your mask and cut it out carefully.

3 To fix on the nose, fold it in half and push the small flaps into the slits you have made. Now you can decorate the mask.

Challenge
Can you make any other features stick out on the mask? Perhaps the crown?

4 Paint the king or queen's face and use gold or silver paint, glitter glue, glue and sequins to decorate the crown. Measure a thin piece of elastic around the back of your head. Cut and attach it to the sides of the mask with a staple on each side.

Challenge
What other characters could you create by changing their headwear?

Egyptian mask

Make a precious gold and blue Egyptian mask like the ancient Egyptians created thousands of years ago.

The ancient Egyptians made masks for their dead pharaohs that they decorated in real gold and with a precious blue stone called lapis lazuli.

✱ This is Tutankhamun's funerary mask. Look at how the blue and gold stripes work together.

✱ How have the eyes and eyebrows been emphasised?

Design and select

Design a mask that looks expensive, exotic and ancient! How much of your face will it cover? Draw your idea and then select your materials. We've used plaster gauze, gold and dark blue paint, and strong elastic.

Make

1 Plaster gauze is very useful for making masks as it moulds easily. You can mould the mask on a friend or get a friend to mould one on you. To stop the plaster sticking, put petroleum jelly over the model's eyebrows, forehead, nose and cheeks — but not on the eyes. Alternatively, you can use a balloon as your mould.

2 Cut the plaster up into small strips. Have a bowl of water close by and cover your work surface with newspaper to protect it. Dip each piece of plaster into the water, hold it over the bowl and squeeze down, pushing out any surplus water and pushing the plaster along in the mesh, filling the holes in the gauze.

3 Layer on the strips of plaster, covering the area around the eyes, down to the end of the nose and across the cheeks. Be sure to leave eye holes. Note: it's important to keep your eyes shut while the plaster strips are on.

4 When you have covered the upper part of the face, leave the plaster to dry for about ten minutes. Once completely dry, remove the mask carefully and paint it with gold paint. When the paint is completely dry, use a fine brush to paint on your decoration in dark blue. Staple some strong elastic to either side to hold the mask on.

Challenge
Could you use plaster gauze to make one of the other characters in this book?

Using your masks

You can use your masks for all sorts of things, including parties, celebrations and decorations. What about putting on a play or mime?

Telling a story

If you decide to put on a play or a mime, think about how you will tell your story. Will you mime to music or to someone reading a story? Consider your audience — will it be mainly children? If so, don't make it too scary!

Choosing your characters

Look at this!

Mime has been performed by various societies for hundreds of years. It is still popular today in places like Andong, Korea, where they hold an annual masked dance festival.

When you produce a play or a mime, think about the characters you will need. How many people will be in it? Will one person play several different characters? You could play a particular piece of music every time a certain character appears. Create an atmosphere by shining torches or spotlights onto the characters.

Ghouls' gallery

You could use your masks to create a themed wall hanging. How about a 'ghouls' gallery' for Hallowe'en or a Japanese display with Noh masks and paper fans? Plan your design on paper first to decide how you will place the masks. Hang them up on string or fix them to a sheet of strong cardboard which you can paint in bright colours.

Party time

Why not have a mask-themed party? You could tell everyone to come in a mask on a set theme or to arrive in any mask they like. Or you could make masks at the party; provide paper, scissors, card, paints and glue and give a prize for the best mask! Whatever you choose, you could make mask-shaped invitations and place cards.

Door decorations

Could you make a self-portrait mask to decorate your bedroom door? Use the pirate mask as a base, but paint yourself on it instead. Stick it on your bedroom door with your name underneath. Alternatively, you could even stick a scary monster mask there with a 'Keep Out, Monsters About' sign beneath! You can easily adapt some of the masks in this book to include your name on the front. For example, why not write your name on the crown of the majestic mask?

Glossary

3D
having three dimensions, length, width and depth

Ancestors
members of your family who lived long before you

Antennae
feelers, aerials

Ceremonies
meetings, celebrations, important or formal events

Exotic
from another part of the world, unusual or glamorous

Funerary
to do with a funeral or burial

Flexible
able to bend

Hallowe'en
31 October, the name is a shortened version of All Hallows' Eve, the day before All Saints' Day

Highwaymen
robbers who stopped carriages at gunpoint to steal from them. They often wore masks to disguise their appearance

Identity
characteristics, personality – who you are

Lapis lazuli
a semi-precious stone, rich blue in colour, often with threads of gold running through it

Metallic
shiny, resembling metal

Mime
a theatrical performance without any speaking

Muzzle
the front part of an animal's face, including the nose and mouth

Noh
classical Japanese theatre which combines dance, drama, music and poetry

Vertebra
a joint in the backbone

Further information

To see some ancient or creative masks, you can visit museums or some art galleries. There are many different types of mask on display at different museums. Check the museum's website or telephone before visiting if you are looking for a particular kind of mask.

Here is a selection of museums that have masks in their permanent collections and on their websites:

The British Museum,
Great Russell Street,
London WC1B 3DG
www.thebritishmuseum.ac.uk

Pitt Rivers Museum,
South Parks Road,
Oxford OX1 3PP
www.prm.ox.ac.uk/masks.html

Cleveland Museum of Art,
11150 East Boulevard,
Cleveland, Ohio 44106
www.clevelandart.org

Milwaukee Public Museum,
800 West Wells Street,
Milwaukee,
Wisconsin 53233
www.mpm.edu

Canadian Museum of Civilisation,
100 Laurier Street,
PO Box 3100, Station B, Gatineau,
Quebec J8X 4H2
www.civilization.ca/indexe.asp

Museum Victoria
GPO Box 666E
Melbourne 3001
Victoria
Australia
www.museum.vic.gov.au

Equipment and craft materials
Stationery, haberdashery and artists' material shops stock most of the materials used in this book.

Index

First published in 2005 by
Franklin Watts, 96 Leonard Street,
London EC2A 4XD

Franklin Watts Australia
45-51 Huntley Street, Alexandria, NSW 2015

© Franklin Watts 2005

Editor: Rachel Tonkin; **Art Director**: Jonathan Hair;
Design: Matthew Lilly; **Photography**: Steve Shott.
Picture credits: Werner Forman/Corbis: 5tl, 22t.
Serge Kozak/Alamy: 12t. José F. Poblete/Corbis: 8t. David
Sanger/Alamy: 28t. Stock Connection Distribution/Alamy: 4bl, 18t.
Roger Wood/Corbis: 4tr, 26t. Every attempt has been made to clear
copyright. Should there be any inadvertent omission
please apply to the publisher for rectification.

A CIP catalogue record for this book is available
from the British Library

Dewey Classification: 731'.75
ISBN 0 7496 6071 6
Printed in Hong Kong/China